Think on Your Feet

Written by Linda Schwartz
Illustrated by Beverly Armstrong

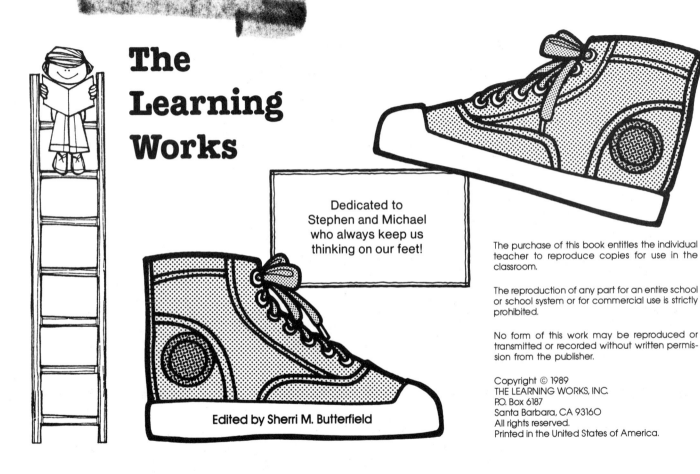

The Learning Works

Dedicated to
Stephen and Michael
who always keep us
thinking on our feet!

Edited by Sherri M. Butterfield

Contents

Introduction 4-6
How to Use This Book 7
When Using This Book for Extemporaneous Speeches 8
Variations for Extemporaneous Speeches 9
Speech Evaluation Form 10
When Using This Book for Creative or Expository Writing Assignments 11
Creative or Expository Writing Evaluation Form 12
Sections
    Just for Fun 13-56
    What If? 57-100
    General Topics 101-140
    Current Issues 141-180
Think up Your Own Just for Fun or What If Topic 181
Think up Your Own General or Current Issue Topic 182
Speaking Award 183
Writing Award 184

Think on Your Feet
© 1989–The Learning Works, Inc.

Introduction

Today's teaching places a strong emphasis on reading, comprehending, memorizing, and repeating facts. Few assignments require students to analyze issues, form opinions, and present their own ideas. As a consequence, kids spend a lot of time learning how to **learn** but very little time learning how to **think**.

Think on Your Feet is a collection of open-ended topics designed to elicit student opinions without requiring extensive background research. Ranging from humorous to serious, these topics make perfect subjects for extemporaneous speeches and for creative or expository writing assignments.

The topics in Think on Your Feet have been divided into four sections: Just for Fun, What If, General Topics, and Current Issues. In general, the topics in the **Just for Fun** section exhibit a touch of whimsy. They require little factual knowledge and lots of imagination.

For example, one topic asks the student to imagine what he would do if he had a tail, and another challenges her to persuade friends to buy a very special chocolate bar she has invented.

Topics in the **What If** section require that the child imagine a situation and elaborate on it. What if you could talk to the president? travel to any country in the world? go back in time and live among the people of any historical period?

Topics in the **General Topics** section require a personal interpretation of specific facts or events. For example, they ask: Which invention has changed your life the most? Do you think that there is life on other planets? What qualities do you look for in a friend?

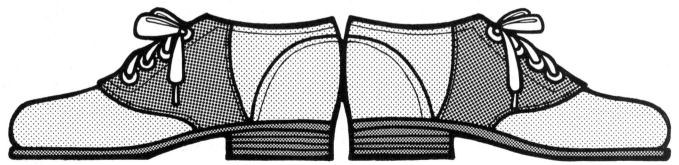

5

Topics in the **Current Issues** section require some knowledge of current events. For example, these topics include questions about AIDS, cigarette smoking, drugs, endangered animals, pollution, school vandalism, nuclear weapons, the use of animals in scientific research, and "pulling the plug." As you can see, these topics may prove to be controversial and will be better managed by more mature students.

Used regularly in your classroom, <u>Think on Your Feet</u> will help students
- clarify values,
- explain opinions,
- express feelings,
- organize and present ideas, and
- gain the confidence needed to speak competently in front of a group.

How to Use This Book

The open-ended topics in <u>Think on Your Feet</u> are perfect for extemporaneous speeches or for creative or expository writing assignments. Of course, to match students with topics, you can simply call names and read topics aloud. But to make this matching process more interesting, photocopy some of the pages from this book, glue these pages to pieces of construction paper or tagboard, and laminate them to make individual topic cards. Sort these cards by book section, topic, or degree of difficulty, and place them in a box of some kind. Make this box available as part of a creative speaking and/or writing center, and encourage students to use it when they "just can't think of anything" to speak or write about.

After you have assigned topics or students have selected them, offer some guidelines for the preparation of written work or oral presentations. For example, you may want to set a word or time limit, and you may need to encourage students to state their position clearly and then to offer three reasons or examples in support of it.

Think on Your Feet
© 1989–The Learning Works, Inc.

When Using This Book
For Extemporaneous Speeches

1. Assign or allow students to select topics.

2. Set a time limit that is compatible with the abilities and attention spans of the students in your classroom.

3. Allow students time in class to think about their topics and to organize their thoughts, but keep preparation time to a minimum.

4. Insist that the actual speech be given **without** notes or visual aids of any kind.

5. At the conclusion of each speech, evaluate the overall presentation (see form on page 10) and, if appropriate, offer suggestions for improvement.

Variations
For Extemporaneous Speeches

1. Rather than working alone, have students work in pairs to prepare oral presentations that will reflect the shared viewpoints of both partners. You may wish to pair students whose oral or organizational skills are well developed with students who are less able in these areas.

2. Videotape oral presentations so that students can observe the areas in which they are especially strong or weak and can learn from their own mistakes.

3. Use topics from the Current Issues section of this book for classroom debates in which individuals or teams take opposing sides.

Think on Your Feet
© 1989–The Learning Works, Inc.

Speech Evaluation Form

5 = **Outstanding**   4 = **Very Good**   3 = **Good**
2 = **Okay But Could Improve**   1 = **Needs Practice in This Area**

Name: _____ Date: _____

Content

1. Began in an interesting and attention-getting manner   _____
2. Stuck to the topic throughout   _____
3. Supported opinion with at least three facts and/or examples   _____
4. Presented facts and/or examples in logical sequence   _____
5. Had a strong ending   _____

Total Number of **Content Points** (possible = 25)   _____

Delivery

1. Stood straight and tall   _____
2. Maintained good eye contact with the audience   _____
3. Spoke in a voice that was sharp and clear, and could be easily heard and understood   _____
4. Varied expression to make the speech interesting   _____
5. Spoke at a pace that was neither too fast nor too slow   _____

Total Number of **Delivery Points** (possible = 25)   _____

When Using This Book
For Creative or Expository Writing Assignments

1. Assign or allow students to select topics.

2. Set a word or length limit that is compatible with your goal for this particular assignment. For example, an early assignment might be to write a single paragraph with a good opening sentence, three or four supporting sentences, and a closing sentence.

3. Allow students time in class to think about their topics and put their thoughts on paper.

4. When students have finished writing, have each one exchange papers with a classmate and proofread the other's work for mistakes in one specific skill area (for example, spelling or use of commas).

5. After students have looked over their own proofread papers and had an opportunity to make any necessary corrections, collect them for evaluation (see form on page 12).

Creative or Expository Writing Evaluation Form

5 = Outstanding   4 = Very Good   3 = Good
2 = Okay But Could Improve   1 = Needs Practice in This Area

Name: _____ Date: _____

Title: _____

1. Title is appropriate. _____
2. Composition has a definite beginning, middle, and end. _____
3. Opening sentence is interesting and attention-getting. _____
4. Main idea is clearly stated. _____
5. Main idea is well supported or explained. _____
6. Words are spelled correctly. _____
7. Punctuation marks are used correctly and consistently. _____
8. Recognized grammar rules are followed throughout. _____

Total Number of **Points Received** (possible = 40) _____

Just for Fun

Think on Your Feet
© 1989–The Learning Works, Inc.

Describe the perfect pet.

What would you do with an **extra** pair of legs?

Think on Your Feet
© 1989–The Learning Works, Inc.

Give a mouth-watering description of a delicious new vegetable you have grown in your organic garden.

Describe the harrowing Halloween
you spent locked
in Mr. Harridan's
abandoned haunted house.

Describe a new sport that will be extremely popular fifty years from now.

You have just invented a device that can be used to brush an alligator's teeth safely. Describe your remarkable invention.

Think on Your Feet
© 1989–The Learning Works, Inc.

Explain to a kindergarten child how to do long division.

What would you do if you had a tail?

9/6/02

What would you do if you had a third eye located in the back of your head?

Create a new toothpaste flavor
that is certain
to please all kids.
Give this flavor a name
and describe
the special toothbrush
you have invented
to go with it.

How would you tell a friend that he or she has bad breath?

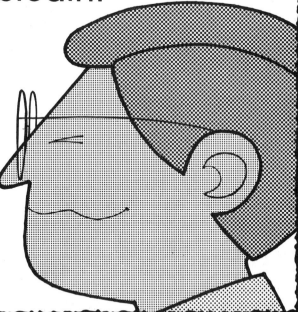

Describe the chaos
in your kitchen
the night the popcorn
would not stop popping.

25

Think on Your Feet
© 1989–The Learning Works, Inc.

Describe an important finding you made while on a recent archaeological dig.

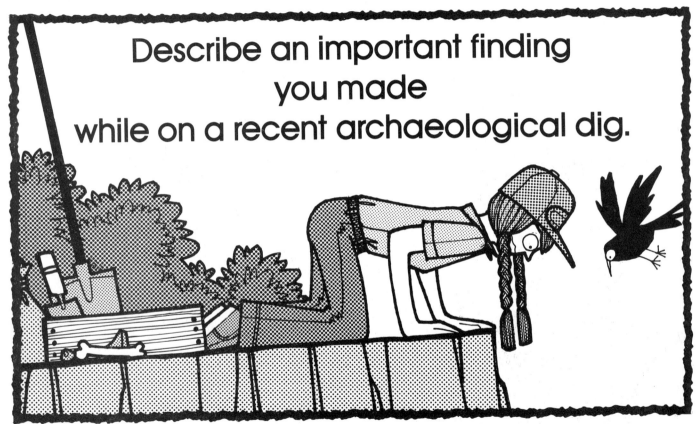

Explain to your teacher
why you did not
do your homework last night.
Create an excuse
you think he or she
has never heard before.

Think on Your Feet
© 1989–The Learning Works, Inc.

Give a step-by-step description of the <u>improper</u> way to prepare for an <u>important</u> final exam.

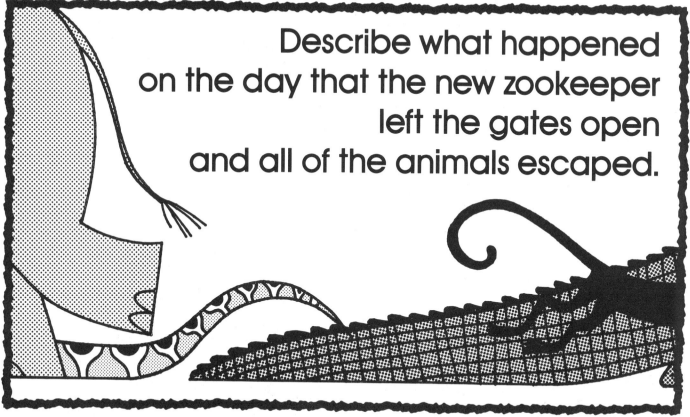

Describe what happened on the day that the new zookeeper left the gates open and all of the animals escaped.

Pretend that you are a freckle on a kid's face.
Tell about your experiences and mention the comments you hear.

Describe an underwater station where humans may live and work in the future.
Tell how the basic human needs for food, oxygen, and water will be met, and describe the areas that will be set aside for work, rest, and recreation.

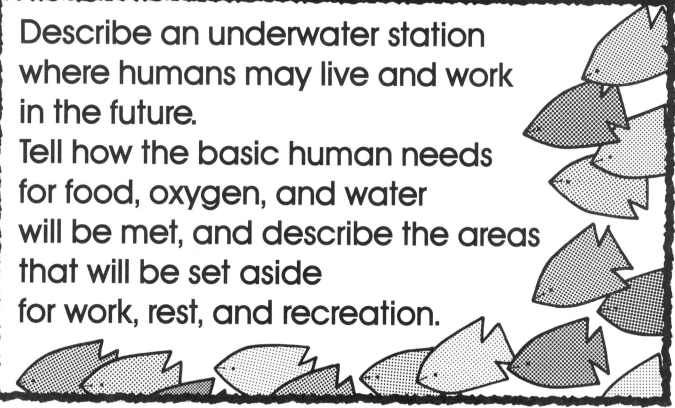

Think on Your Feet
© 1989–The Learning Works, Inc.

Describe your life as an ant at a family picnic.

You have recently built a computerized robot that does homework. Explain how you will go about marketing this device to kids— and to their parents.

Think on Your Feet
© 1989–The Learning Works, Inc.

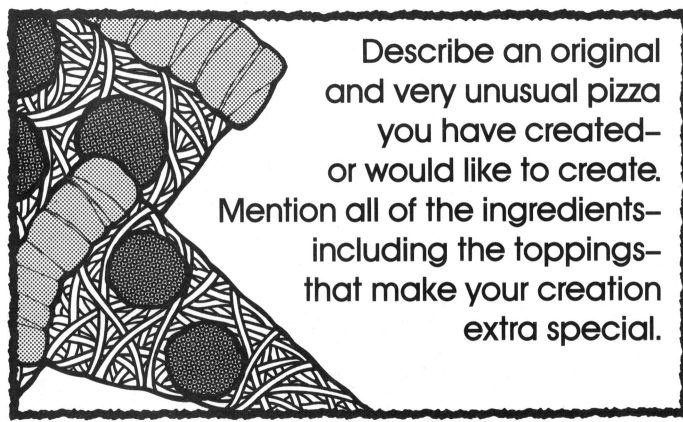

Describe an original and very unusual pizza you have created— or would like to create. Mention all of the ingredients— including the toppings— that make your creation extra special.

Tell about
the most embarrassing moment
of your life.

What would you like to invent to make your life easier or to improve its quality?

What do you think
that you will be doing
with your life
twenty-five years from now?

Describe a very unusual sandwich you have created all by yourself, even if it is only in your imagination.

You are about to spend two months
alone on a deserted island.
There is plenty of food and water.
Name five other things
you will take with you
and explain why you chose each one.

Think on Your Feet
© 1989–The Learning Works, Inc.

Describe a magic potion
you have discovered
and tell about the special powers
that it has.

The faces of four presidents
are carved in the rocks
of Mount Rushmore in South Dakota.
What if you could choose
three more people to immortalize
in the stone of this mountain?
Whom would you pick and why?

Think on Your Feet
© 1989–The Learning Works, Inc.

Create a new curriculum
for the grade you are in.
What old subjects
will you eliminate?
What new subjects will you add?
In what ways will you revise
the old subjects that you keep?

HISTORY OF SPORTS

Propose a new law that kids your age would have to obey. Explain why your law would be beneficial.

A Hollywood movie director wants to make a movie based on your life. Describe the scene that will be your favorite and tell who should be hired to play the part of <u>you</u>.

Convince your friends to buy a chocolate bar you have just invented.

ULTRAFUDGE

A HUNK OF CHOCOLATE IN YOUR POCKET!

Create a new event
for the Summer or Winter Olympics.
Briefly describe
the rules for this event
and tell what special clothing
and equipment participants will need.

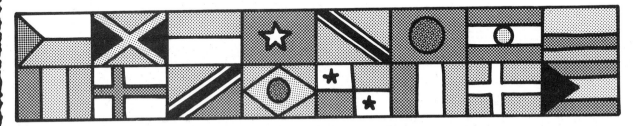

Describe the worst gift
you ever received.

Think on Your Feet
© 1989–The Learning Works, Inc.

Describe in detail
the perfect treehouse
for you and your friends.

What would you do if you had an extra set of hands?

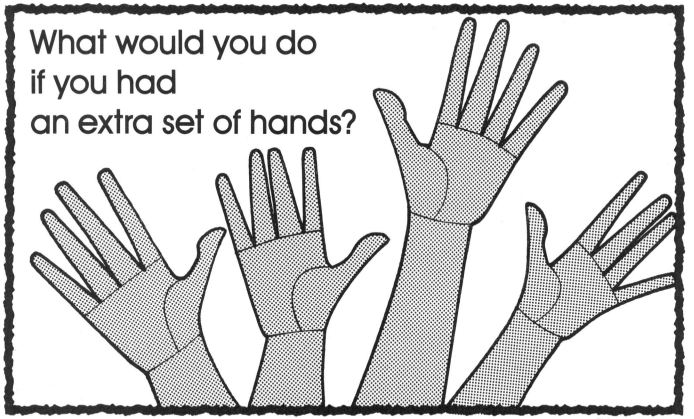

Describe a new amusement park attraction that combines monsters, water, and a roller coaster ride.

EEEEEYAH!

What arguments
would you give your mom and dad
so that they would let you
keep a tarantula as a pet?

Think on Your Feet
© 1989–The Learning Works, Inc.

Disneyland is divided into different theme areas, such as Adventureland and Fantasyland. What if you were chosen to design a new theme area for this amusement park? What would you call your new theme area? What rides and/or attractions would it contain?

SWAMPLAND!

Describe a more modern
super hero
who might replace
Tarzan of the jungle.
What special powers
would this new hero possess?

Think on Your Feet
© 1989–The Learning Works, Inc.

Tell how you would get out of eating a vegetable that you hate so that you could have a dessert that you love.

Describe the funniest thing that ever happened to you while you were on vacation.

Think on Your Feet
© 1989–The Learning Works, Inc.

Do you think that there is life on other planets?

What If?

What if you were one of a group of sextuplets? Describe a typical morning at your house.

What if you received a gift
of one thousand dollars cash?
What would you do
with the money?

Think on Your Feet
© 1989–The Learning Works, Inc.

What if you were a door?
Would you want to be the door
to a bank, to a castle,
to a haunted house,
to a kid's treehouse,
or to some other kind of building?
Describe the kind of door you would be
and the experiences you might have.

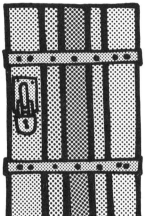

What if you awoke one morning to find yourself completely invisible?

Think on Your Feet
© 1989–The Learning Works, Inc.

What if your teacher gave you a grade of C on a paper you had written? If you believed you deserved a better grade, how would you go about convincing your teacher to change it?

What if you were one of the first astronauts to land on Planet Perfecta in the Milky Way galaxy? Describe this perfect place to live.

Think on Your Feet
© 1989–The Learning Works, Inc.

What if you woke up one morning to discover that all of the numbers had disappeared? In what ways would your life be different?

What if
Martin Luther King, Jr.,
were alive today?
In what ways might
things be different?

What if you could be
any animal for a day?
Which animal would you
choose to be and why?

What if you could travel to any country in the world with all expenses paid? What country would you choose? Why?

PERU CHINA FRANCE INDIA SCOTLAND AUSTRALIA

What if you could acquire one skill,
such as the ability to draw,
to play the piano,
or to perform a gymnastic routine?
Which skill would you choose?
Why?

What if you woke up one morning to discover that you had the powers of Superman? How would you use these special powers?

70

What if you were
a visitor from Mars?
Pick a place
to land your spacecraft
and describe earthlings
from an alien's
point of view.

What if you could be famous
for one special thing
as an adult, such as
finding the cure for a disease,
performing as a rock star,
or doing something else important?
What one thing would you
choose to be famous for and why?

What if you could
not talk or whisper
for an entire week?
Describe the ways in which
you would communicate
with others.

What if you could be a hat
sitting on someone's head?
What kind of hat would you be?
Would you belong to an astronaut,
a fire fighter, a football player,
a miner, a pilot, the president,
a queen, a sailor, or someone else?
Describe your experiences as a hat.

What if you were
in a department store
and saw someone shoplift?

Think on Your Feet
© 1989–The Learning Works, Inc.

What if everyone on earth spoke the same language?

What if there were no oceans, rivers, or seas on the earth?

ATLANTIC PRAIRIE

PACIFIC DESERT

What if you got the measles every time you touched anything that was the color red?

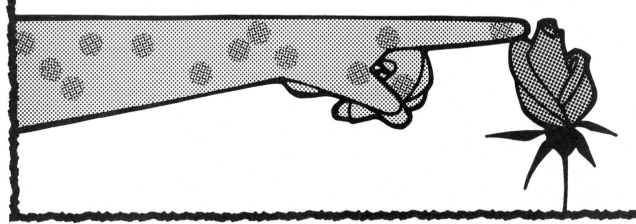

What if you could change your name? What new name would you pick? Why?

				JIM	NATHAN	THED
				JOHN	NICK	TIM
				JOSEPH	PAUL	TOM
				JUSTIN	PETE	TONY
				KEN	PHIL	WALT
				KIETH	RANDY	WILL
				KYLE	RAY	
ADAM	BEN	ED	HAL	LANCE		
ALAN	BOB	ERNIE	HANK	LARRY		
ALEX	CHARLIE	FRANK	JACK	LOU	RO	
ANDY	CHUCK	GENE	JAMES	MARK	ROG	
ARTHUR	DAN	GERALD	JASON	MATT	SAM	
BART	DENNIS	GREG	JEFF	MIKE	STEVE	

79

Think on Your Feet
© 1989–The Learning Works, Inc.

What if there were no trees or flowers on the earth?

What if you were a shoe?
Would you want
to be a ballet slipper,
a cowboy boot, or some
other kind of footwear?
Describe your experiences
as a shoe.

Think on Your Feet
© 1989–The Learning Works, Inc.

What if you could talk with the president of the United States in a three-minute telephone conversation? What would you talk about? What questions would you ask?

What if you could go back in time and live among the people of any historical period, such as the knights of the Middle Ages or the pioneers of the Gold Rush? Which people and period would you choose?

What if everyone in your neighborhood looked exactly alike?

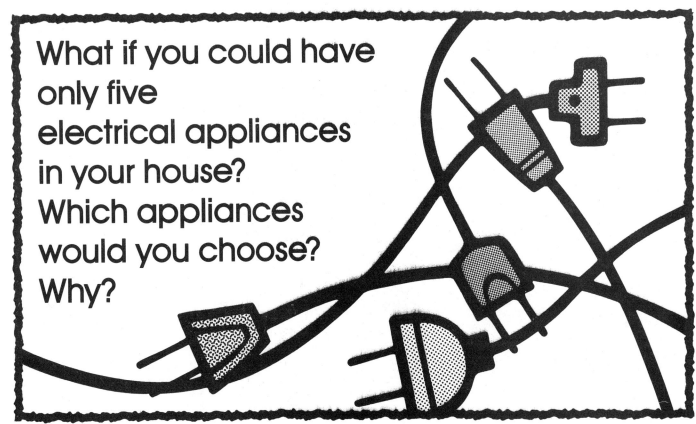

What if you could have only five electrical appliances in your house? Which appliances would you choose? Why?

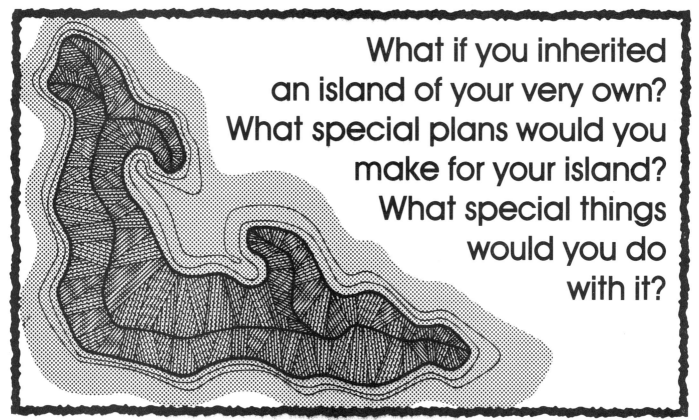

What if you inherited an island of your very own? What special plans would you make for your island? What special things would you do with it?

What if you could go back in history and change the outcome of one important event? Which event would you choose to change? Why? In what ways would you change it?

JFK Survives Dallas Assassination Attempt

What if everyone lived
to the ripe old age of 175?
In what ways
would life on earth
be different
with this longer
life expectancy?

Think on Your Feet
© 1989—The Learning Works, Inc.

What if all
of the television sets
in the world disappeared?
How would your life
be different?

What if you found out
that you had
only one year
to live?
What would you do
with the time
you had left?

March
April
May
June
July
August
September
October
November

What if you could change three things about the world? What changes would you make?

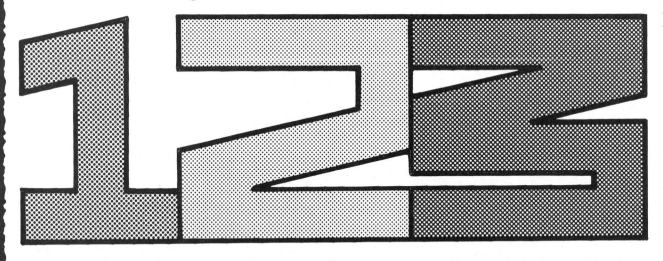

What if you could invite
any famous person to lunch?
Whom would you select and why?
What would you talk about?

What if you could invent a new breakfast food that kids would prefer to eggs or cereal? Describe this breakfast treat.

What if you
were the school janitor
for a day?
Tell what changes
you would make.

Think on Your Feet
© 1989–The Learning Works, Inc.

What if you could give
ten thousand dollars
to any nonprofit organization?
Which group would receive
your money?

What if you were
not required by law
to attend school?
If you chose not to attend,
how would you spend
your days?

What if one of your parents was critically ill? What things would you do differently at home?

Think on Your Feet
© 1989–The Learning Works, Inc.

What if tomorrow was declared National Backwards Day? Describe how you would observe this special day from night until morning.

What if you could climb between the covers of any book and become a character in the story? What book would you choose and which character would you be?

General

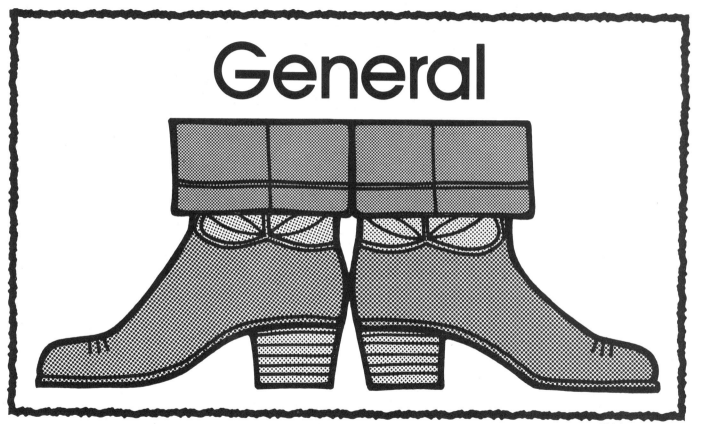

Think on Your Feet
© 1989–The Learning Works, Inc.

Describe the best movie you have ever seen.

1. ALLOWANCE
2. BEDTIME / CURFEW
3. JOBS AND RESPONSIBILITIES
4. SPECIAL PRIVILEGES
5. TRADITIONS
6. VALUES

In what ways would you raise your children differently from the way in which your parents raised you?
In what ways would you raise them the same?

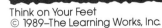

Describe the color of happiness.

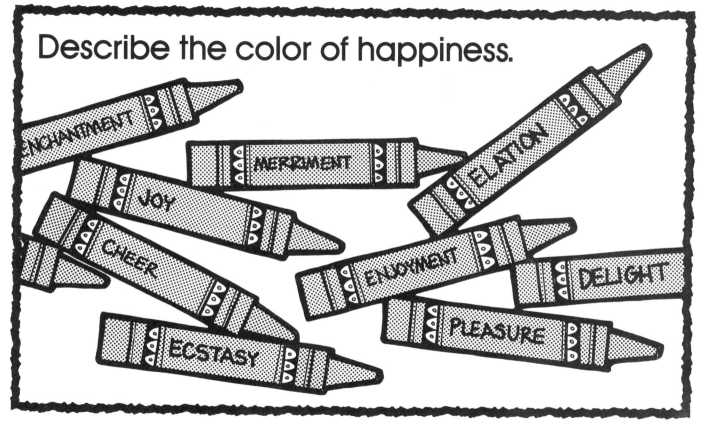

Think on Your Feet
© 1989–The Learning Works, Inc.

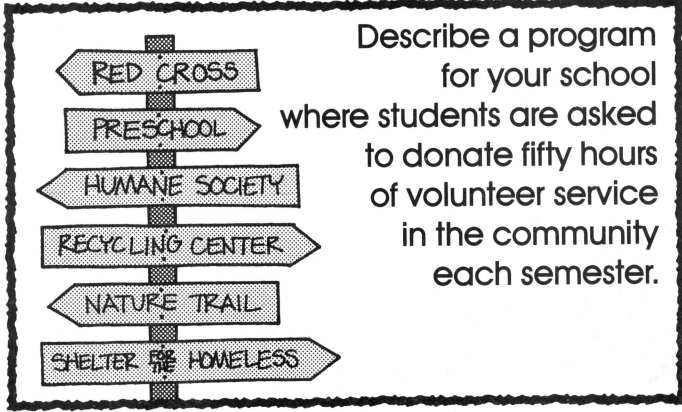

Describe a program for your school where students are asked to donate fifty hours of volunteer service in the community each semester.

If you had a week to spend all by yourself indoors, how would you spend it?

Describe what you would do if you discovered that marijuana was being smoked at a classmate's party.

Do you think
that watching television
has helped or hurt kids?
Support your viewpoint
with specific examples.

109

Tell about an unforgettable day in your life.

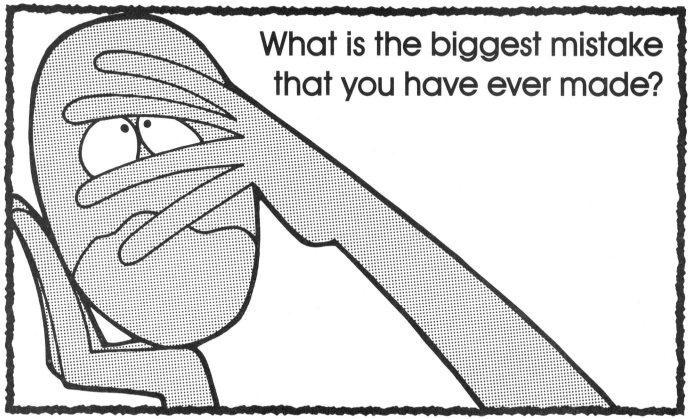

What is the biggest mistake
that you have ever made?

111

How do you measure success?

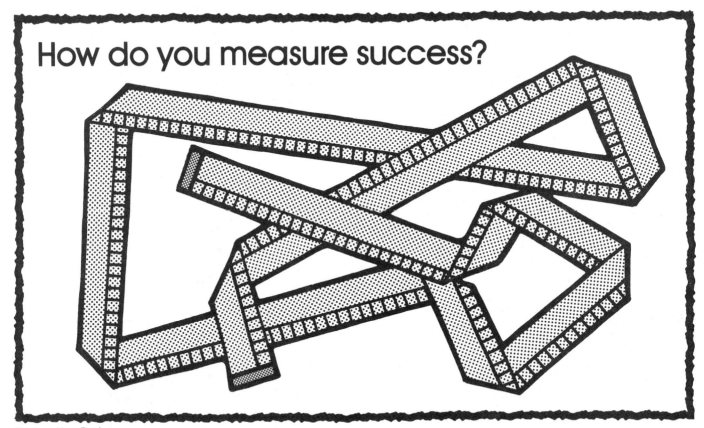

Describe the perfect teacher.

Think on Your Feet
© 1989–The Learning Works, Inc.

Describe the color of hate.

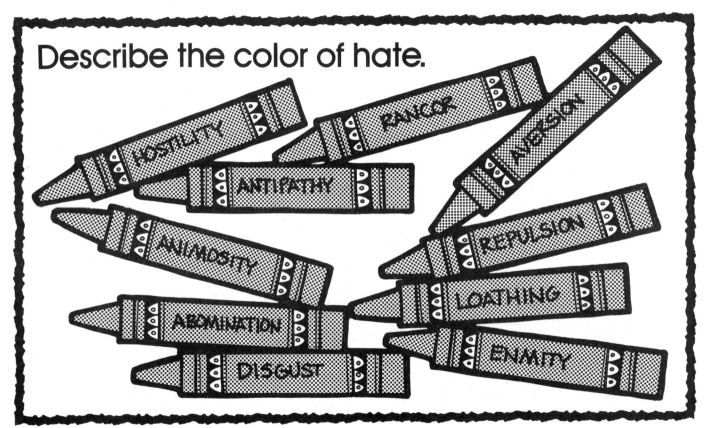

What are some of the things that you hope to accomplish by the time you are fifty years old?

Think on Your Feet
© 1989–The Learning Works, Inc.

If you had a week to spend all by yourself outdoors, how would you spend it?

Describe the ways in which your life would be different if you were confined to a wheelchair.

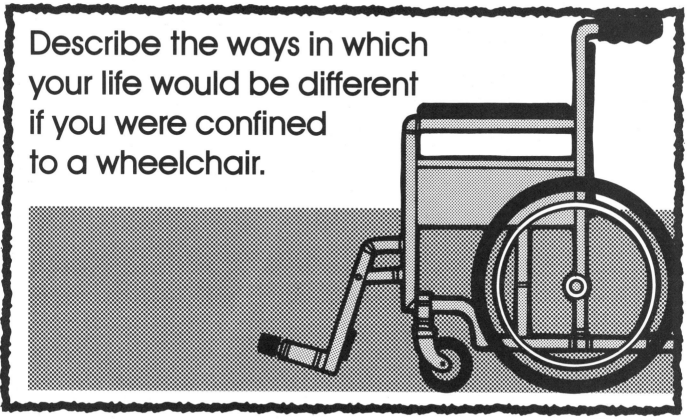

Think on Your Feet
© 1989–The Learning Works, Inc.

What are some special events, both good and bad, that have happened to you?

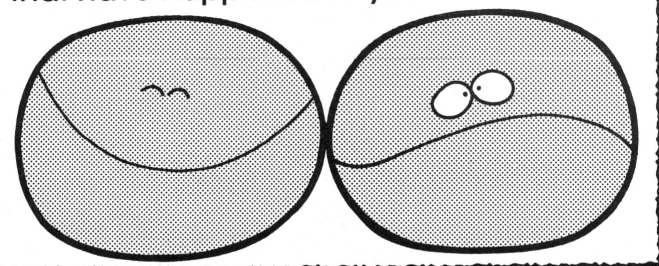

Describe a relative who is very special to you.

Aunt Pat & I

Would you rather be an only child, the youngest child, or the oldest child in a family?

Describe a turning point in your life.

Think on Your Feet
© 1989–The Learning Works, Inc.

What is the best age to be?

Describe the best book you have ever read.

Describe a serious disagreement
you had with a close friend,
a brother, a sister,
or your parents.
Tell how you
settled the matter.

Think on Your Feet
© 1989–The Learning Works, Inc.

How would you convince
a good friend
to quit smoking
cigarettes?

Convince your parents to give you the raise in allowance which you believe you deserve.

What are your five
most treasured possessions?
Why is each one of them
special to you?

Think on Your Feet
© 1989–The Learning Works, Inc.

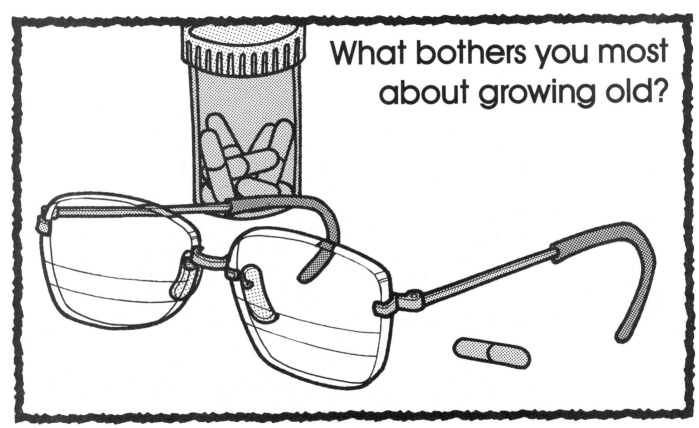

What bothers you most about growing old?

Which invention has changed your life the most?

Describe what you would do if you saw a classmate cheat on a test.

Do you think that women who are full-time homemakers do a better job of "mothering" than women who work outside the home?

What is creativity?
Give examples of people
who are creative
and of things
that embody this quality.

If you were killed
in an accident,
would you want
your parents to donate
your heart, liver,
or retinas
to save the life or sight
of another child?

What was one
of the proudest moments
in your life?

Think on Your Feet
© 1989–The Learning Works, Inc.

SUPER CITY
POPULATION
1,537,282

WEST SUBURBIA
5 MILES ⇨

← FARMTOWN • 23 MILES

Do you think
it would be more fun
to grow up on a farm,
in the city,
or in the suburbs?

What advice would you give to parents to help them get along better with kids your age?

SUGGESTIONS

Think on Your Feet
© 1989—The Learning Works, Inc.

Describe a person who has had a positive influence on your life.

What is the hardest thing you ever had to do?

What do you think schools will be like in the year 2100?

Current Issues

If your parents' marriage was in trouble, would you rather have them stay together with tension and fighting or get a divorce and break up the family?

Do you believe that there is life after death?

Think on Your Feet
© 1989–The Learning Works, Inc.

Should teachers be allowed to spank disruptive students?

What is the
most serious problem
facing our country today?

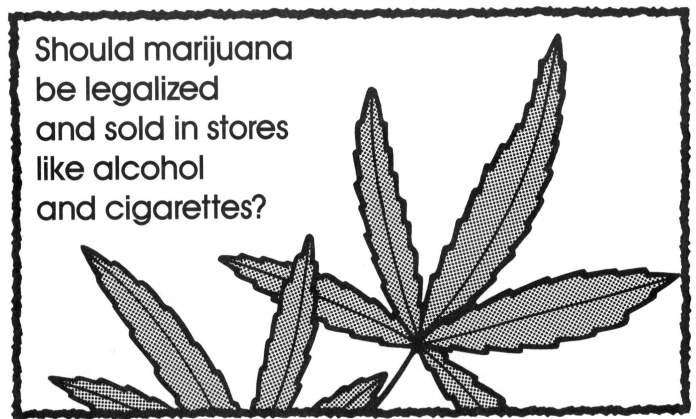

Should marijuana be legalized and sold in stores like alcohol and cigarettes?

How should teenagers who are caught vandalizing a school be punished?

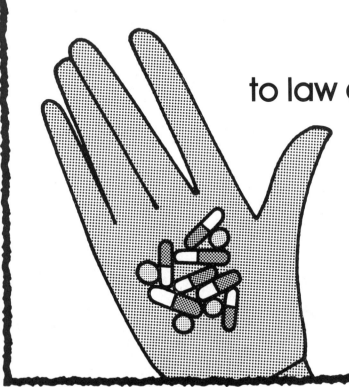

Would you turn in a close friend to law enforcement officials if you discovered that he or she was selling drugs to other children in your school?

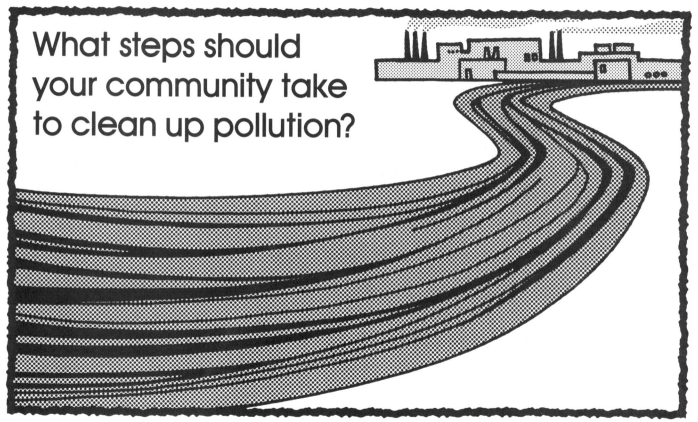

What steps should your community take to clean up pollution?

"Latchkey children" is a term used to describe kids who return to an empty house after school because both of their parents work. What can be done to ensure the safety of these kids after school?

Should high school students be allowed to smoke cigarettes on campus in designated areas?

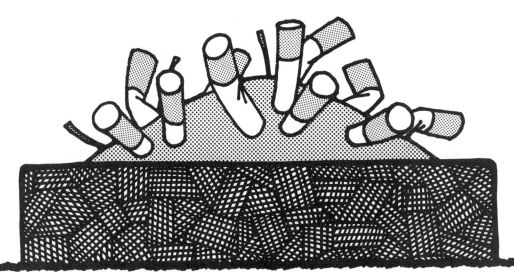

Tell why you think
that a woman
would or would not be
as good a president
as a man.

Think on Your Feet
© 1989–The Learning Works, Inc.

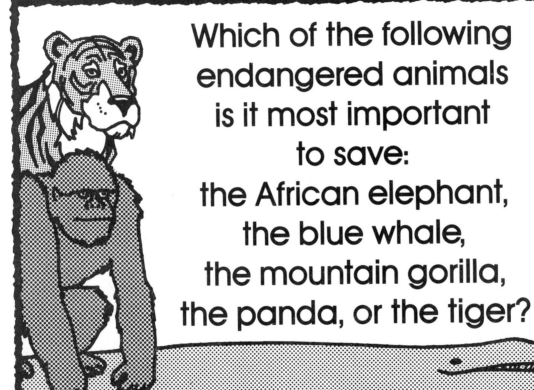

Which of the following endangered animals is it most important to save: the African elephant, the blue whale, the mountain gorilla, the panda, or the tiger?

Should our government pass a law limiting the number of children each family can have?

Think on Your Feet
© 1989–The Learning Works, Inc.

What steps should your community take to prevent pollution?

How should people who are convicted of drunk driving be punished?

Should schools enforce strict dress codes that prohibit extreme styles of makeup, hair, or dress?

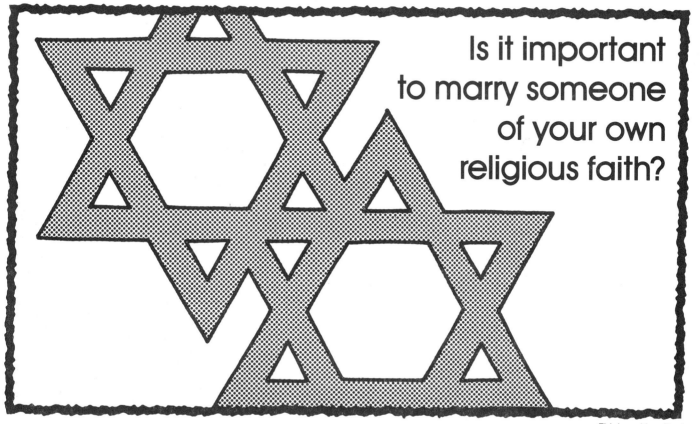

Is it important to marry someone of your own religious faith?

Think on Your Feet
© 1989–The Learning Works, Inc.

Should kids who have been infected with the AIDS virus be allowed to attend public schools?

Which one of the following freedoms is most important to you: academic freedom, economic freedom, political freedom, or religious freedom?

Does our country need stronger gun-control laws?

Think on Your Feet
© 1989–The Learning Works, Inc.

Should two years of foreign language study be required in elementary school?

hormiga

cocodrilo

mariposa

If a person is terminally ill with no chance of recovery and is being kept alive by a life-support system, should a family member be allowed to "pull the plug"?

Think on Your Feet
© 1989–The Learning Works, Inc.

Should more money be spent on finding a cure for AIDS, cancer, or heart disease?

Today, many communities face the problem of overcrowded jails. How would you feel about having a minimum-risk prison built in your neighborhood?

Should religious holidays, such as Christmas and Hanukkah, be celebrated in public schools?

What can be done
to stop kids
from dropping out
of high school?

Should schools follow a year-round schedule, where students attend classes during the summer months and have several two- or three-week vacations throughout the year?

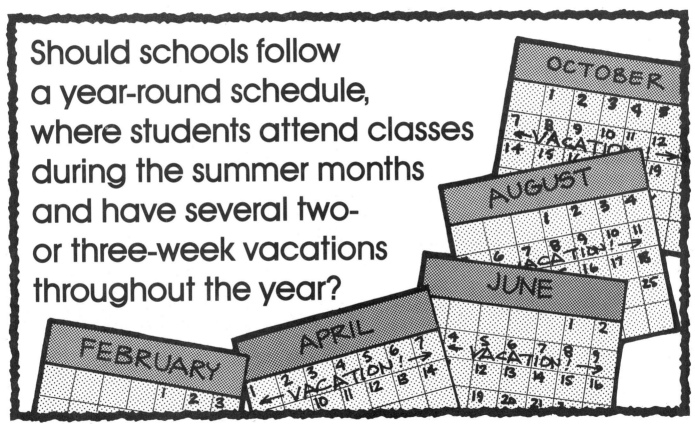

Should the death penalty be abolished?

In what ways might you and your friends help the poor and needy in your community?

Should scientists test drugs and conduct experiments on animals to advance medical research?

Think on Your Feet
© 1989–The Learning Works, Inc.

If students vandalize a school, should their parents be held financially responsible for the damage?

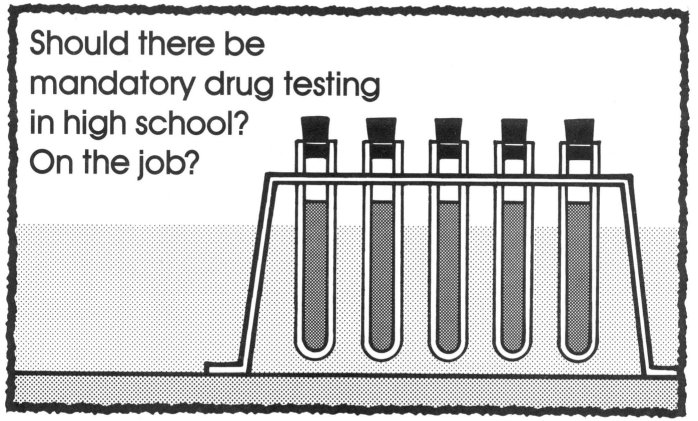

Should there be mandatory drug testing in high school? On the job?

Think on Your Feet
© 1989–The Learning Works, Inc.

If one of your parents was addicted to cocaine, would you turn him or her in to authorities in an effort to help?

Should helmets be required
for all people
who ride motorcycles?

In what ways could the people running our government do a better job?

Should our government spend more money on education, the environment, national defense, the poor, or space exploration?

What is
the most serious problem
on your school campus?

Think up Your Own
Just for Fun or What If Topic

_____

_____

_____

_____

_____

_____

Think on Your Feet
© 1989–The Learning Works, Inc.

Think up Your Own
General or Current Issue Topic

_____

_____

_____

_____

_____

_____
(name)

Your talk was grrrreat, and so you rate this very special

Speaking Award.

_____
(signature)

_____
(date)

Writing Award

for

_____
(name)

When you write that well, it's fun to read. Thanks!

_____
(signature)

_____
(date)